APRIL
FOOL'S FUN

By
Mary E. Hirsch

What Is April Fool's Day?

The first day of April is called April Fool's Day. How this day began for sure is not known although most people believe it started a long time ago in France. At that time the first day of the year was March 25 and New Year's Week was the week before April 1st. That week was always filled with fun and festivals much like New Year's Eve and New Year's Day is now.

But eventually the King of France decided to change the first day of the year to January 1st. Not everyone liked the change, and not everyone could remember the change had taken place. These people continued to celebrate the first week of April as the first of the year. They were known as April Fools for thinking it was New Year's Day.

Now everyone celebrates January 1st as the first day of the new year, but April 1st is still a special day; a day when people act like "fools" by playing jokes on one another. For tricksters, spoofsters, magicians, jokesters and other fun people, April 1st is always a great day because they get to do what they like to do -- play tricks. This book has lots of ideas for tricks you can play on April Fool's Day. Just remember, tricks should be fun not mean, and if you are going to play tricks on others you have to be ready to have tricks played on you.

April Fool's Day will be twice as fun if you laugh not only at others but at yourself.

April 1st
New
Year's Day

Happy April Fool's Day!

Tricks To See

People who see us almost everyday don't look at us very closely. (I'll bet you can't remember what color shoes your teacher had on yesterday.) A slight change in your appearance may go unnoticed for a very long time and makes for a great April Fool's trick. Here are some things you can do to change how you look. See how many people notice the change and how long it takes for them to see it.

- Wear two different shoes.
- Wear your shirt inside out.
- Wear two different colored socks.
- Roll up one leg on your pants or one arm on your shirt.
- Put purple or green dots on your hands (be sure to use washable markers!)
- Put two different colored shoelaces in your shoes.
- Wear only one earring or two different earrings.
- Wear your slippers instead of your shoes.
- Put the wrong initials on your shirt.
- Use a string or piece of yarn instead of a belt.
- Put a piece of macaroni through a string and wear it as a necklace or bracelet.

Backwards Say To Things
(That's April Fool Talk For Things
To Say Backwards)

Think of some things you say to different people during the day. Write them down, then practice saying them backwards so you'll be ready to use them. Here are a few good ideas to get you started:

* Johnson Mrs. morning good.
* Dinner for what's?
* Pencil a borrow I can?
* Lunch for bring you did what?
* Today nice very look you.
* Letter a mail to like I'd.
* Friend my your glad I'm.
* Homework my with me help you could?
* Notebook my take you did?
* Joke a hear to want?
* Book a find me help you can?
* Is it time what know you do?
* Gum some like you would?
* Practice baseball to going you are?

Others any of think you can?

OOOOOOM, OOOOOOM

Tricks To Play On Others

One of the great traditions of April Fool's Day is to play practical jokes on people. These jokes should be fun but not hurt anyone. One common joke is to call the zoo and ask for Mr. Bear or Mrs. Lion. In fact a lot of zoos have a special tape recording they play when they get calls like that so they can play a joke on the joker.

Here are some tricks you might want to try. But remember, good tricksters know that a trick or two might be played on them so if you are going to play tricks be ready to have a laugh on yourself sooner or later.

- Tie a string to a coin purse. Leave it on the sidewalk and hide behind some bushes. When someone comes to pick it up, pull it away.

- Put a long piece of green yarn in a handkerchief and then pretend to blow your nose. Pull away the handkerchief and let the yarn fall down.

- Put double sided tape or another sticky substance on a dime and put it on the floor or on top of your desk at school. When someone tries to pick it up, it will be stuck and you can watch them try to pull it off.

- Say "What's that on your face?" to your friends; when they say "Where" and feel their face you can say "It's your nose; didn't you know you had one?"

- Put your pajamas on over your clothes and go to breakfast. Tell your family that this is what you are going to wear today. When they say you can't wear that say "April Fools" and take off your pajamas.

- Take cotton balls and wrap them in colored tissue paper or tin foil. Ask your friends if they would like some candy. After they open the trick candy and find cotton, you can say "Hey haven't you ever heard of cotton candy?"

- Put a couple of pillows on your bed and cover them up with your blanket. When someone comes in to your room to see if you are up you can hide and watch them as they try to wake up your pillows.

- Run a string through the arms of your jacket or sweater and hang some old mittens stuffed with newspaper or paper hands you cut-out at both ends of the string. Then put your own hands inside your arms and let your new hands hang around.

- Tell your friend that you can jump over two feet. Then jump over his two feet.

- With a friend stand on the sidewalk or playground and look up at the sky, pointing and saying things like "Wow," or "I've never seen anything like that!" or "What do you think it is?" Watch while other people come over and start looking up to see what you are looking at. When they finally ask you what it is say "It's a spaceship full of April Fools, like you!"

- Put confetti and cotton balls in a cup that you can't see through. When someone comes along act like you are drinking from the cup. As the person gets closer hold out the cup like you are offering them a sip. Then pretend to trip and throw the cotton balls and paper on them. They'll think you are going to get them all wet and will jump away.

April Fool Rules

April Fool's Day is a time when everything is a little bit crazy. The usual rules don't always count. Below are some crazy, mixed-up rules. Can you think of others? What are some of the rules you have at home or school?

- Brush your meals after every teeth.
- Look both streets before you way the cross.
- Cover your sneeze when you mouth.
- If can't nice something say then don't something at all say.
- Don't in the runs hall.
- Don't mouth with your talk full.
- Clothes up your hang.
- Don't nose your pick.
- Never strange to talkers.
- Don't with play matches.
- Do others unto as you have would others you do.

Trick Questions To Ask Others

Trick questions are ordinary questions that we turn into tricks by thinking about them in a different way.

Did you take a bus today?
  (Yes)
Well give it back!

Is your refrigerator running?
  (Yes)
Well you better catch it.

Did you take a bath last night?
  (Yes)
Well you must be very strong to be
able to lift it up!

Have you ever eaten soup with a sandwich?
  (Yes)
Really! I always have to use a spoon.

Is your television working?
  (Yes)
What kind of job does it have?

Are you smart?
  (Yes)
Nice to meet you Smart, my name is _____.

Want to hear a secret?
  (Yes)
Whisper in their ear: "A Secret."

Tricky eMails And Letters

Another fun trick is to write crazy notes to your friends, family, teachers and sign them with April Fool names.

Some names you could use are:

- Prell Fool
- O.N. Lee Fooling
- Ima Fooling
- Ima Kiddin
- Itza Trick
- Itza Joke
- Joe King
- U. B. Tricked
- Bea N. Silly
- Ben A. Fooling

There are lots of notes you can write. The sillier and wilder the better. Here are a few ideas:

Dear Dad:
I gave your car to the Goodwill. Love
A. Prell Fool.

Dear Letter Carrier:
Please sing Jingle Bells when you deliver our mail.
Itza Trick

Dear Teacher:
I ate my homework for breakfast. It was very
good with milk and sugar and I should get an A for it.
Ben A. Fooling

Dear Mom:
All my teeth fell out. Can we have soup for dinner?
Joe King

Dear Molly:
After school let's go to the moon. I have a rocket at my house and we can be back in time for dinner. I want you to meet the moon people who are my friends.
U.B. Tricked

Dear Grandma:
How are you? I am fine. My ears turned purple and fell off but that's okay because our new green pig Marvel ate them after she baked a chocolate cake for her boyfriend Kevin Kamel. I am doing well in school except for when I ate my desk and put oatmeal in my teacher's shoes because I thought they were cereal bowls. Tonight I am going to Mars on a spaceship with my new polka dotted alien friends Spugzoli and Wenstogol. I will be back soon.
Love,
Jimmy
P. S. Happy April Fools Day

April Fools Cards

There are Valentine's Day cards, Christmas cards, Birthday cards so why not make your own April Fool's Day Cards. Here are some different types of cards you can make and sayings to write on them.

Fold a piece of paper in half and then glue it shut. After it has dried, write on the front and back. The person you give it to won't be able to open it. Some ideas for the cards are:

FRONT: I just sent this card to say...
BACK: Have a Happy April Fools' Day.

FRONT: You're so wonderful, You're so cool
BACK: You also are an April Fool.

FRONT: If you can open this card in two seconds you'll win a prize!
BACK: Oh well...Happy April Fools' Day.

FRONT: There's $500 inside this card...
BACK: APRIL FOOLS!

Put a little surprise in the card for your friend:

FRONT: This is the kind of card that will really...
INSIDE: BUG YOU (Draw or paste pictures of bugs all over the inside)

FRONT: There is a lot of money inside this card.
INSIDE: Write "A LOT OF MONEY" all over the inside of the card

FRONT: What does an April Fool look like?
INSIDE: A lot like you I guess! (Tape a piece of tin foil inside with a frame around it like a mirror)

FRONT: I got a band to play just for you.
INSIDE: Have a rubber band taped inside with the instructions "Pull very fast."

Fold a piece of paper in half. Write normally on the cover and then write upside down on the inside. For instance:

FRONT: What kind of cake do you eat on April Fool's Day?
INSIDE: Upside down cake.

FRONT: I'm not going to try to trick you on April Fools'
Day...
INSIDE: Unless you open this card!

FRONT: Knock, Knock
       Who's There?
       Turnover
       Turnover Who?
INSIDE: Turnover this card if you want to read it.

April Fool Jokes To Tell

What would April Fool's Day be without some jokes to tell?
Here are a whole day and a half full of jokes for you to use.

Where do you go to learn practical jokes?
>April Fools' School

What does a funny carpenter wear?
>A fool belt.

Where does a jokester keep her ice cream?
>A fooler cooler.

What do you all a comical monster?
>An April Ghoul.

Where do pranksters get all wet?
>They jump into the swimming fool.

Why are goats so much fun?
>They're always kidding around.

What's inside an egg laid by a funny chicken?
>A joke-yoke.

What is a trickster's favorite vegetable?
    The Artijoke.

What does a comedian drink who wants to lose weight?
    A Diet Joke.

What plantgrows in the Funny Forest?
    Poison joke.

What is Wacky Wrestler's favorite move?
    A joke hold.

Why was the prankster so cranky in the morning.
    He just joke-up.

What does a Western comedian call his children?
    Little cowjokes.

What is an April Fool's favorite dance?
    The Hokey-Jokey.

Where's the wackiest place to climb to?
    On top of Old Jokey.

What is funny, brown and lives in the woods?
　　Jokey the Bear.

Where do cranky people sit in restaurants?
　　In the No Joking Section.

What is the funniest city in the world?
　　In Jokyo.

What is the funniest state?
　　Idaho-ho-ho

Why wouldn't the dog laugh in the backyard?
　　He was housejokin'.

What is a comedian's favorite game?
　　Joker Poker.

Who do you sell old riddles to?
　　A Pawn Joker.

How do you make bad jokes disappear?
　　Say Jokeus-Pocus.

Why was the photographer so sad?
> His camera was out of jokeus.

What has feathers, lives on a farm and performs magic?
> A trickin' chicken.

What does a magician eat her food with?
> Choptricks.

Why are hockey players like magicians?
> They all want to have hat tricks.

What is big, gray, swims in the ocean and does magic?
> Moby Trick.

What is Funny Freddy's favorite toy?
> A Pogo Trick.

Why did Magic Matthew have to take a lot of baths?
> He was always doing dirty tricks.

What magic show do mice like to watch?
> Tricky Mouse.

What did Colonel Sanders say to the magician?
> "Your show was finger trickin' good."

Why is a leaky faucet so much fun?
> It is always doing trickles.

What is a prankster's favorite piano song?
> Choptricks.

What is green and full of surprises?
    A Dill Trickle.

How do you make a magician laugh?
    You trickle his feet.

What does a prankster eat when she's hot?
    A popsitrickle.

What did the April Fool say to his watch dog
when some crooks tried to break in?
    Trick 'em Rover.

What did the robber say when he held up the magic store?
    This is a trick-up.

Why was the prankster holding her breath?
    She was trying to get rid of the trick-ups.

What is a prankster's favorite nursery rhyme?
    Hickory Trickery Dock.

What did the foolish chef cook on April 1st?
    Silly Chili.

Why wouldn't the April Fool go on an ocean cruise?
    He was afraid he'd get set trick.

What do you call pranksters who live in the mountains?
    Silly hillbillies.

What animal is the biggest fool?
    An Ape-ril Fool (but I'm not going to be the one to tell him!)

What do you call a rabbit born on April 1st?
    A funny bunny.

Why did the doctor make Giggling Gail laugh?
    Because she was fixing her funny bones.

Why was the pencil laughing?
    It was writing on the funny papers.

What's the happiest animal at the zoo?
    The Gir-laugh.

Why did Silly Sam eat a joke book?
    He wanted a few belly laughs.

And, of course, there are always some great Knock-Knock jokes too:

Knock Knock
        Who's there?
Justice
        Justice who?
Just us April fools.

Knock Knock
        Who's there?
Joe
        Joe Who?
Joe-Ker.

Knock Knock
        Who's there?
Who
        Who Who?
Why why are you
you talking talking like
like that that?

Knock Knock
        Who's there?
Ape
        Ape who?
Ape-ril Fools, no one's here!

End The

So have a happy holiday.

Happy Holidays

I mean have a great Halloween:

I mean

APRIL FOOL'S

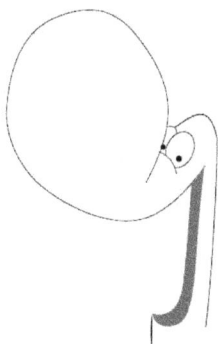

www.ingramcontent.com/pod-product-compliance
Lightning Source LLC
Chambersburg PA
CBHW060608030426
42337CB00019B/3672